# OBSERVING THE ]
# MOON

## JOHN S. FOLKES

**For my grandson Daniel**
**who loves the Moon**

HarperCollinsPublishers Ltd.
77–85 Fulham Palace Road
London
W6 8JB

The Collins website address is:
www.collins.co.uk

Collins is a registered trademark of
HarperCollinsPublishers Ltd.

First published in 2003

09 08 07 06 05 04 03

10 9 8 7 6 5 4 3 2 1

A catalogue record for this book is available from the
British Library.

ISBN 0 00 715431 3

Designed by Colin Brown

Printed and bound in Great Britain by Bath Press

# CONTENTS

# 01 TELESCOPIC INSTRUMENTS

## INTRODUCTION

It is still less than a century ago that the American astronomer Edwin Hubble first proved beyond doubt that galaxies lay far beyond the Milky Way, and that subsequently it was discovered that the Universe was expanding. Since this time, and with the aid of modern telescopes, space probes and computer technology, our understanding of how the Universe works has been considerably enhanced.

What is not always readily appreciated is that much of the basic knowledge about the heavens had been gathered and recorded centuries before the first telescope made its appearance. During this time people had always studied the planets and their apparent motions, the 'wanderers' we now call comets, the patterns made by the stars, the Moon, and the Earth itself in relation to its neighbours.

The remarkable thing is that some of this knowledge was uncannily accurate. Eratosthenes (275–195 BC), a Greek mathematician, geographer and astronomer, not only demonstrated that the Earth is a globe but measured its circumference with a precision that is truly outstanding. He also estimated the size of the Sun and the Moon and calculated their approximate distances from us. The crater named after Eratosthenes is featured in this book as object number 16 (see chapter 2). It is equally remarkable that the Maoris of New Zealand knew about the rings of Saturn and had knowledge of Jupiter's moons. They passed this information down through the centuries as part of their legends. Yet there is no mention of anything like a telescope in their history. How they knew this is one of the unsolved mysteries of antiquity, as it is impossible for the human eye to resolve anything as faint as Saturn's rings.

The scientific community had to wait to study the heavens in detail until October 1608, when Jan Lippershey, a Dutch spectacle maker, applied to the Netherlands government to patent a telescope and news of the device reached Galileo Galilei in 1609. It was this great Italian physicist and astronomer who pioneered telescopic observation of the heavens.

## CHOOSING THE RIGHT TELESCOPE

The astronomical instruments which are available today for the amateur astronomer would be the envy of past observers, but the overwhelming choice can still prove to be a minefield. If the wrong choices are made, images will not live up to expectations.

So, as an observer what sorts of instrument are we looking for? The answer to this question depends on where your main observing interests lie. Ask yourself whether you are most likely to be doing deep-sky observing or lunar and planetary observing.

Generally speaking, there are two types of telescopes – the **refractor** and the **reflector** – and this choice can be extended to include a variation of the reflector design known as the Cassegrain. Each is based on the same principle: to gather as much light as possible from an object, and bend the light to a point called a *focus* at which an image of the object is produced. This image is then magnified until it can be seen with the human eye. The part of the telescope which gathers and focuses the light to reproduce the original image is called the **objective lens** or **mirror**. The part which magnifies the image is called the **eyepiece**.

The relationship between the lens or mirror and its effective aperture is known as the **focal ratio** or $f/$ number. The $f/$ number determines what kind of observing the instrument is best suited to. For example, a $f/5$ 12 inch (30.5cm) mirror will have a focal length of 60 inches (1520.5mm).

In practical terms the higher the $f/$ number the better it is in resolving fine detail and, therefore, the better suited for planetary or lunar observing. Short-focus telescopes ($f/5$ and below) are best suited for observing deep-sky objects. These figures are only a guide, as there are many variations in telescopic design and so a compromise is often necessary.

With the refracting telescope, the objective lens is located at the front of the tube. Light passing through the lens is bent inwards until it comes to a focus at the far end of the tube and the eyepiece picks up the image at this point.

**REFRACTOR**

The design and development of the reflecting telescope was first presented to the Royal Society in 1671 by Sir Isaac Newton and the basic design is still used today throughout the world. The determined pioneer observer William Herschel, on the 13th March 1781 using a 7ft (214cm) reflecting telescope from his back garden in the city of Bath, discovered what was later to be confirmed as the planet Uranus.

The reflecting telescope is characterised by a reflecting mirror as primary and a diagonal secondary mirror, positioned to reflect the light rays through 90° to a focus near the side and towards the open end of the telescope tube.

**NEWTONIAN REFLECTOR**

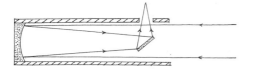

In 1672, shortly following Sir Isaac Newton's successful development of the mirror-based telescope, a variation of the reflecting telescope, called the Cassegrain telescope, was invented by the French astronomer, Cassegrain. Using a concave primary mirror, it reflects the light rays up to a convex secondary mirror. These light rays are then reflected back down through a hole in the primary mirror to the so-called **Cassegrain focus** below.

**CASSEGRAIN**

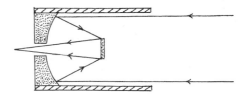

Although large reflecting telescopes dominate observatories throughout the world, refractors are nevertheless a widely used instrument and are preferred by many observers. The basic design and method of fixing their optical components mean they are inherently less likely to go out of alignment, unlike those of a reflector. The unobstructed light path and enclosed tube assembly generally contribute to a better and steadier image than those produced by a comparable-sized reflector. What gives the refractor quality of image with minimum distortion is the design of the type of lens that it uses. This is because when a beam of white light passes through a simple lens, the white light is split up into the various colours so that each colour comes to a slightly different focus. The result is that the image of any object produced by the lens is surrounded by false-coloured fringes or 'false colour'. To counteract this undesirable effect, known as **chromatic aberration**, the refractor uses compound lenses in both the objective lens and eyepiece. This comprises several elements manufactured from glasses having different dispersion properties. It is the type of lens used in the construction of a refractor and is known as an 'achromatic lens'.

Many of the observations in this book were carried out using a modest 60mm refractor. Although too small to resolve in detail images of *craters* and *rille* systems, the small refractor is ideal for becoming acquainted with lunar features and prominent formations, such as the mountain range Montes Jura, the Bay of Rainbows, and many more besides.

There is no question that the larger the instrument, the better the results. However, if siting the telescope is limited in terms of physical space, then portability has to be the major factor in deciding what instrument to purchase. Given the criteria on the relationship between the lens or mirror and its effective aperture size, then with higher *f/* numbers and larger apertures there will be a corresponding lengthening in tube size. Consequently, there will be a considerable increase in the instrument's sphere of influence when turning it through 360°. Remember that you will be operating the equipment under dark conditions.

Before making any final decision about which instrument to buy, you will have to consider local conditions such as quality of view, for example. Is the pathway of the planets (the *ecliptic*) obstructed by trees or buildings? You will also have to assess light pollution, such as street lighting, flood lights and security lighting systems. The performance of even the best instrument will be seriously compromised if any of these factors are present – again, something portable would seem to be the best option when purchasing a new instrument. The Newtonian reflecting telescope uses what is called a parabolic mirror surface, which reflects the light falling upon it. Just before a point known as **prime focus** a small flat mirror set at 45° intercepts the reflected light from the mirror and directs a cone of light outside where it is passed through an eyepiece. The reflecting telescope has given good service to many amateur observers and can be relatively cheap to buy.

So far we have only considered the telescope itself, but of equal importance is the type of mounting to which the telescope is attached. Generally, there are two types of instrument mounting designs: the **Altazimuth** and **Equatorial**. The Altazimuth can be considered as a general-purpose mounting suitable for attaching binoculars or wide-field instruments where tracking is not necessary. Where tracking is required

then we can encounter many different mechanical systems using an Equatorial mounting.

All telescope mountings must be constructed to have motion about two axes and at right angles to each other. When one these is mounted to align with the rotational axis of the Earth, then to follow a star the telescope only has to move in the other axis. This aligned axis is called the **polar axis** and is pointed at the **Celestial Pole**. Depending on the latitude location of the observer, the instrument's polar axis could range from being vertical at the Pole to horizontal at the Equator. The other axis is called the **declination axis** and is used to turn the telescope up and down the sky away from the polar orientation.

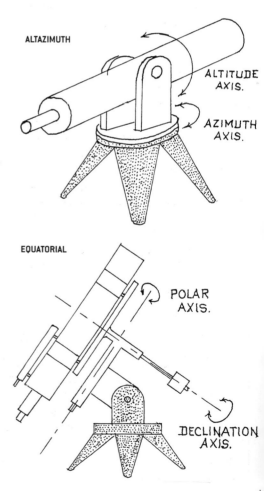

**ALTAZIMUTH**

ALTITUDE AXIS.

AZIMUTH AXIS.

**EQUATORIAL**

POLAR AXIS.

DECLINATION AXIS.

Modern computerised telescopes have been able to dispense with traditional mounting systems as they can drive both axes at the same time in order to remain fixed in relation to the night sky. Planetary and lunar tracking require a separate drive rate in order to remain fixed in relation to the target's motion. Separate drive rates are normally featured in the more expensive telescopes. Some observers using the Newtonian design find the eyepiece position awkward and tiresome to use. The Cassegrain design not only yields high magnification with a short tube and an eyepiece that may be reached comfortably, but it is also compact and easy to use.

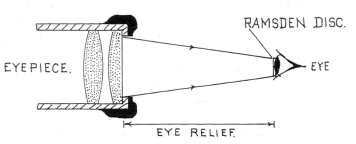

## EYEPIECES

The purpose of the eyepiece is to magnify the image formed by the objective lens or mirror. As this book concerns itself with lunar observing, we need only to identify those eyepieces which are going to produce the best observing images. Due to the nature of the lunar terrain, one of the main characteristics which we are looking for in the eyepiece design is **contrast**, another is **resolving power**. This resolving power of an eyepiece is its ability to pick out detail in an image (in the book you will find references to 'resolving images'). To do this, we often need to increase the magnification, but if we use more than we need to separate detail, we degrade the clarity of the image rather than enhance it.

**Plössl eyepiece sizes suitable for lunar observing**

| Diameter | Eye Relief Range | Focal Length Range |
|---|---|---|
| 1.25 inches – 31.7mm | 4mm to 25mm | 4mm to 40mm |

Selecting the eyepiece size we require from the available range in focal lengths, and using the conversion table below, we can calculate the magnifying values we require against the appropriate mirror or objective size. For example, a 6 inch (15.25cm) *f*/8 mirror or objective lens will produce an overall system focal length of 1220mm. To calculate the magnification value, divide the eyepiece focal length into the system's overall focal length. Therefore, using a 40mm focal length eyepiece with a 6 inch (15.25cm) *f*/8 mirror will produce a magnification of 30×. Using a 4mm focal length eyepiece with a 6 inch (15.25cm) *f*/8 mirror will produce a higher magnification value of 305×.

**Conversion table**

| Mirror or Objective Diameter | *f*/ Value of Mirror or Objective Diameter in Millimetres | | | | | | |
|---|---|---|---|---|---|---|---|
| | *f*/4 | *f*/5 | *f*/6 | *f*/7 | *f*/8 | *f*/9 | *f*/10 |
| 3 inch – 7.5cm | 300 | 370.5 | 450 | 520.5 | 600 | 670.5 | 750 |
| 4 inch – 10cm | 400 | 500 | 600 | 700 | 800 | 900 | 1000 |
| 6 inch – 15.25cm | 610 | 760.25 | 910.5 | 1060.75 | 1220 | 1370.25 | 1520.5 |
| 8 inch – 20cm | 800 | 1000 | 1200 | 1400 | 1600 | 1800 | 2000 |
| 10 inch – 25.5cm | 1060 | 1270.5 | 1530 | 1780.5 | 2040 | 2290.5 | 2250 |
| 12 inch – 30.5cm | 1220 | 1520.5 | 1830 | 2130.5 | 2440 | 2740.5 | 3050 |

A factor we have to consider when using eyepieces is what is known as the **exit pupil**. Imagine the light rays leaving the objective as a cylinder of light. Passing through the optical elements in the telescope, the light rays are bent into a cone until they emerge from the eyepiece where the cylinder of light has been considerably reduced. This emergent cylinder of light rays is called the exit pupil, and its cross section is known as the **Ramsden disc**. The exit pupil is important because of its relationship with the eye itself. Depending upon the brightness of the daytime light, the pupil of the eye will vary in size from 2mm to 4mm. At night, however, the eye pupil expands to 7mm or 8mm. An exit pupil of 7mm, therefore, cannot possibly enter the eye during daylight, and consequently that part of the emergent beam of light is wasted. This is a consideration you may take into account when viewing the Moon at the full *phase*. As the exit pupil consists of light from the whole surface area of the mirror, cutting off the outside portion of the exit portion is equivalent to reducing the size of the mirror. If the exit pupil is 8mm and eye pupil is 4mm, the effectiveness of the mirror is reduced by half. On the other hand, if the exit pupil is only 1mm or 2mm, much of the potential of the eye is wasted during night-time observing.

Finally, we have to consider the distance from the outer surface of the eyepiece lens to the Ramsden disc. This measurement will provide us with what is known as **eye relief**.

There is a generous range of eye relief to choose from in eyepieces, from 4mm to 25mm, providing the observer with a comfortably obtained and unobstructed field of view, and of particular importance if you have to wear spectacles.

It is recommended that for lunar observing a minimum requirement of two eyepieces would be needed: a low-magnification 1.25 inch (31.7mm) Plössl eyepiece with a eye relief value of the observer's own choosing and a Barlow lens which increases the magnification of the telescope typically 2×. Only at a later stage when experience is gained in lunar observing would introducing a high-magnification Plössl to your armoury be advisable, particularly if the telescope does not have a lunar drive rate, because the higher the magnification the quicker the lunar image moves across the field of view.

## SUMMARY

What governs your choice of instrument is determined by how much you are willing to spend, the space you have available, and the conditions which prevail in the location where you are operating the telescope. You may wish to delay making the final choice by joining a local astronomical society. This way you can discuss and draw on the experience of like-minded observers to guide you through the finer aspects of observing and, at the same time, get hands-on experience by using their equipment initially.

## INTRODUCTION

The Moon seen through the eyepiece of a telescope is every bit as spectacular as it is varied, in both its appearance and wealth of detail. The *synodic month* (lunar month) reveals a changing moonscape with its dramatic contrast between light and dark, and advancing and retreating shadows, presenting the observer with an endless array of challenges.

From the safety and comfort of the eyepiece the observer can escape the harsh reality and extremes of the lunar seasons, with solar winds bearing an endless bombardment of cosmic rays and temperature variations of 273°F in full sunshine in the lunar summer to minus 244°F in the lunar winter.

We are fortunate to enjoy the company of our closest celestial neighbour and the Solar System's fifth largest satellite. That first-time glimpse through the eyepiece of a telescope never fails to invoke a response of 'Wow!', and yet for the most part we take it for granted and only occasionally make time to study its ever-changing features. To take full advantage of those rare occasions when atmosphere, cloud conditions and opportunity permit us to observe the Moon, it is vital to prepare in advance what object we are going to observe and where it is located.

First quarter, full moon, last quarter and new moon are *phases* with which we are all familiar, and predicting their arrival is straight forward. However, if we are going to increase our understanding of the Moon's features we need to have at hand a greater accuracy of information to predict where and when the individual objects can be seen at their best time. Just as important is knowing the next exact occasion on which we can observe that object under the same lunar conditions in case we were to miss the opportunity to observe, for whatever reason.

It is with this in mind that the lunar calendar can be consulted, and the *terminator* position can be predicted on a daily basis. This enables you to choose objects for observation at predictable times, days, weeks, months, or even years in advance. Any creditable Moon map is ideal for this purpose and essential as a reference point when both selecting and confirming observations.

When observing, having the right tool for the job is essential, so choosing the right eyepiece is important. As a general rule, a low magnification is all that is necessary to study chosen objects and their surrounding terrain. Only choose higher magnification if viewing conditions permit, otherwise it will not resolve fine detail and the results will be disappointing. Naturally, observing through the eyepiece will present a different orientation of image than to the naked eye, so this consideration must be a part of the preparation process. For example, if the image is inverted (upside down and back to front) through the telescope, then familiarise yourself with the Moon map placed upside down, where the object will be seen in its proper orientation and in context with neighbouring features.

For ease of comparison, each of the illustrations that accompany the observation features in this chapter includes a scale and is drawn in its normal orientation of north and south.

# RECOMMENDED VIEWING FEATURES

The following features include a cross section of *craters*, *maria*, mountains, *scarps* and a network of *rilles*, totalling over one hundred objects, which include a selection of Apollo landing sites. All features are described and illustrated in this chapter, except where indicated.

| Lunar Day | Object Number | Feature |
|---|---|---|
| 1 & 16 | 1 | ONE-DAY-OLD MOON |
| 3 & 17 | 2 | THREE-DAY-OLD MOON |
| 4 & 18 | 3 | CAPELLA |
| | 4 | FRACASTORIUS |
| 5 & 19 | 5 | STATIO TRANQUILLITATIS |
| | 6 | THEOPHILUS |
| 6 & 20 | 7 | ARISTOTELES |
| | 8 | EUDOXUS |
| | 9 | JULIUS CAESAR |
| 6 & 21 | 10 | LINNE – no drawing |
| 7 & 22 | 11 | VALLIS ALPES |
| | 12 | TRIESNECKER |
| | | FIRST QUARTER |
| 8 & 23 | 13 | PLATO |
| | 14 | ARCHIMEDES |
| | 15 | PTOLEMAEUS |
| 9 & 24 | 16 | ERATOSTHENES |
| | 16 | STADIUS |
| 9 & 23 | 17 | SCHRÖTER |
| 9 & 24 | 18 | BIRT |
| | 19 | TYCHO |
| | 20 | CLAVIUS |
| 10 & 25 | 21 | COPERNICUS |
| | 22 | BULLIALDUS |
| 11 & 26 | 23 | SINUS IRIDUM – no drawing |
| | 24 | LANSBERG |
| 12 & 28 | 25 | MAIRAN |
| 12 & 27 | 26 | KEPLER |
| | 27 | GASSENDI |
| 13 & 28 | 28 | ARISTARCHUS |
| | 29 | SCHICKARD |
| 14, 27, 28, 29 | 30 | DESCRIPTION OF MAIN FEATURES |
| 15 | 31 | FULL MOON |
| | | LAST QUARTER |

*Above*: This photograph shows the locations of the lunar features 2–29 described in this chapter. The numbers relate to the object numbers in the table opposite. The numerical sequence of these selected features follow the natural movement of the terminator from east to west. They have been illustrated with an easterly oblique lighting effect, in order to enhance the natural contours of the features as they are seen through the eyepiece.

To observe the features of the Moon, the observer needs to know the position of the *terminator* at any given moment. For this purpose, tables for calculating terminator values are usually given in astronomical almanacs.

To simplify what can be a lengthy process of calculation, we can refer to the lunar day calendar to help work out the best viewing times for any given lunar feature. For example, the *crater* 'Stadius' (object 16) will be in view when the Moon is 9 and 24 days old. To convert this to celestial observing time, we need to refer to the new moon phase calendar (see below). To observe crater Stadius in June 2007, we note that the new moon occurs on the 15th. Adding this celestial date figure to the lunar days 9 and 24 we can determine that Stadius (object 16) will be best placed for observing on the 24th June with the lunar day 24 spilling over into 8th July.

| NEW MOON PHASE CALENDAR | | | | | |
|---|---|---|---|---|---|
| | **2003** | **2004** | **2005** | **2006** | **2007** |
| JANUARY | | 21 | 10 | 29 | 19 |
| FEBRUARY | | 20 | 8 | 28 | 17 |
| MARCH | | 20 | 10 | 29 | 19 |
| APRIL | | 19 | 8 | 27 | 17 |
| MAY | | 19 | 8 | 27 | 16 |
| JUNE | | 17 | 6 | 25 | 15 |
| JULY | | 17 | 6 | 25 | 14 |
| AUGUST | | 16 | 5 | 23 | 12 |
| SEPTEMBER | | 14 | 3 | 22 | 11 |
| OCTOBER | 25 | 14 | 3 | 22 | 11 |
| NOVEMBER | 23 | 12 | 2 | 20 | 9 |
| DECEMBER | 23 | 12 | 1 & 31 | 20 | 9 |

**Note:** For new moon phase dates beyond 2007 contact NASA Reference Publication 1349 Planetary Ephemeris website at: http://lep694.gsfc.nasa.gov/code693/TYPE/TYPE.html

# SELECTING LUNAR FEATURES FOR OBSERVATION

To find the best observing time for lunar features other than those given in this book, obtain the longitude value of the terminator position and match it against the nearest longitude setting in column 1.

The adjacent column 2 will tell you what lunar day it falls on. Following the instructions below accompanying the new moon phase calendar you can determine its best viewing date.

## GUIDE TO POSITION OF TERMINATOR AND AGE OF MOON

| COLUMN 1 Terminator Position in Longitude | COLUMN 2 Lunar Day | COLUMN 1 Terminator Position in Longitude | COLUMN 2 Lunar Day |
|---|---|---|---|
| 61°E | 1 | 55.8°E | 16 |
| 47°E | 2 | 43.5°E | 17 |
| 36.8°E | 3 | 33.5°E | 18 |
| 27.5°E | 4 | 24.5°E | 19 |
| 19°E | 5 | 16.2°E | 20 |
| 10.8°E | 6 | 8.2°E | 21 |
| 3°E | 7 | 1°E | 22 |
| 4.5°W | 8 | 7°W | 23 |
| 12.5°W | 9 | 15.2°W | 24 |
| 20.7°W | 10 | 23.7°W | 25 |
| 29°W | 11 | 32.2°W | 26 |
| 39°W | 12 | 42°W | 27 |
| 49.6°W | 13 | 54.5°W | 28 |
| 64°W | 14 | 70°W | 29 |
| 73°E | 15 | | |

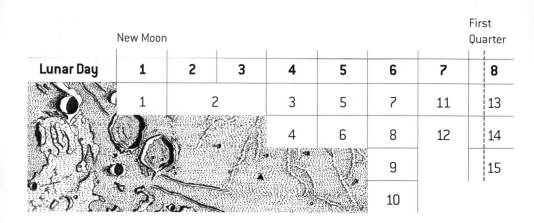

|  | New Moon | | | | | | | First Quarter |
|---|---|---|---|---|---|---|---|---|
| **Lunar Day** | 1 | 2 | 3 | 4 | 5 | 6 | 7 | 8 |
|  | 1 | 2 | | 3 | 5 | 7 | 11 | 13 |
|  | | | | 4 | 6 | 8 | 12 | 14 |
|  | | | | | | 9 | | 15 |
|  | | | | | | 10 | | |

|  | | | | | | | Full Moon |
|---|---|---|---|---|---|---|---|
| **Lunar Day** | 9 | 10 | 11 | 12 | 13 | 14 | 15 |
|  | 16 | 22 | 24 | 26 | 29 | 31 | 32 |
|  | 17 | 23 | 25 | 27 | 30 | | |
|  | 18 | | | 28 | | | |
|  | 19 | | | | | | |
|  | 20 | | | | | | |
|  | 21 | | | | | | |

The Moon's orbital journey around the Earth contrasts with a backdrop of starry constellations. Although close to the *ecliptic*, the Moon's path has a maximum variation of about 5° either side.

When observing the Moon, bear in mind that starting from the new moon phase the Moon will in fact travel eastward relative to the Sun through 90° arriving at the first quarter phase and becoming visible in the evening sky. At the full moon phase the Moon's apparent eastward motion places it on the opposite side of the sky relative to the Sun's position, appearing to us at about sunset and shining through-

| Lunar Day | 16 | 17 | 18 | 19 | 20 | 21 | 22 | Last Quarter<br>23 |
|---|---|---|---|---|---|---|---|---|
| | 1 | 2 | 3 | 5 | 7 | 10 | 11 | 13 |
| | | | 4 | 6 | 8 | | 12 | 14 |
| | | | | | 9 | | | 15 |
| | | | | | | | | 18 |

| Lunar Day | 24 | 25 | 26 | 27 | 28 | 29 | New Moon |
|---|---|---|---|---|---|---|---|
| | 16 | 22 | 24 | 27 | 26 | 29 | |
| | 17 | 23 | 25 | 28 | | 30 | |
| | 19 | | | | | 31 | |
| | 20 | | | | | 32 | |
| | 21 | | | | | | |

out the night. Relative to the Sun, the Moon's continuing motion places it 90° west of the Sun's arriving at the last quarter phase where it rises at midnight to be visible in the early-morning sky.

Note that between the ecliptic and the celestial sphere there is an angle of 23° 26' 27" known as 'obliquity of the ecliptic'. Together with the Earth's eccentric motion around the Sun, this not only provides us with our seasonal changes, but means that the new moon phase will vary in altitude above the horizon throughout the year, depending on where in the world you are observing.

### Object 1: THE ONE-DAY-OLD MOON (also visible on Lunar Day 16)

Probably the most difficult phase to observe is when the Moon is one day old. This is due to its very slender crescent and low altitude. Coupled with the low brightness of the Moon itself and high brightness of the sky, it makes a very difficult challenge to the observer.

Despite the aforementioned problems, features are visible on the thin crescent. The largest crater visible is the **Mare Humboldtianum** (Humboldt's Sea) [57°N, 80°E].

The eastern edge of this feature extends to longitude 90°E and hence its visibility is much affected by *libration*. Mare Humboldtianum is the dark flooded centre of a lunar basin with a concentric outer wall approximately 640km in diameter. The diameter of Mare Humboldtianum is approximately 160km and it occupies an area of 22,000km².

As the day progresses, another thicker dark streak – but only about two thirds as long – should appear between Humboldt and the terminator: this is the crater **Phillips** [26.6°S, 76.0°E], 124km in diameter. Appearing as a continuation to the north of Humboldt is a much darker shadow, which is the east wall of **Hecataeus,** 127km in diameter. North again is a shorter black streak, the crater **Behaim**, 55km in diameter. Finally, two black specs can be seen; the southern is **Ansgarius**, 94km in diameter, and the lighter northern one is **Lapeyrouse**, 78km in diameter. Humboldt crater itself has a fractured floor, a massif 207km in diameter and relatively flat, giving a clue perhaps to it being filled with volcanic lava or impact melt. After solidification, this filling of the crater fractured irregularly either because of contraction, subsidence of the crater floor, or volcanic intrusions beneath the crater floor.

Moving north from Lapeyrouse, covering a distance around twice that of from Humboldt to Lapeyrouse, we find another dark dash, which is the crater **Plutarch**, 68km in diameter. To the north of this is **Gauss** – a mountain-walled plain over 177km in diameter. This is a difficult, but not impossible object to observe using a telescope. The above craters will be seen as narrow long ellipses, with perhaps faint irregularities. With binoculars, however, you will observe only black and dark streaks and smears because you only see their most illuminated regions, the dark shadowed inner east walls. Their bright, illuminated inner west walls are lipped away from us, and the bright floors blend in with the surrounding light areas.

Alexander von Humboldt (1769–1859), was a German naturalist and explorer. In South America in 1799 he observed the Leonie's meteor shower. He went on exploratory expeditions to the (then) little-known rivers Orinoco and Amazon, and to the Andes, Mexico and Siberia. Mädler gave Humboldt's name to the mare because he recognised a symbolic parallel between Humboldt's explorations of unknown terrestrial continents and the way that this lunar feature seems to form a link between the known and unknown hemispheres of the Moon.

*Above*: The Moon seen at three days old

The three day old Moon offers the observer a full and complete sunlit crescent. Added to this, the light reflecting onto the Earth from the crescent creates a visible darkened outline of the remaining lunar disc, known as 'earthshine'. It is at this stage that the observer will be able to see the unfolding images to their best advantage, that is to say with minimum glare from the narrow sunlit crescent, sandwiched as it is between the terminator and the darkened sky beyond the Moon's eastern limb.

Even at this early stage in the synodic month, the Moon offers over 40 sites to observe, providing us with a complex and diverse range of black, shadowy contours. These are abstract in appearance and are constantly changing into what will eventually become familiar regional moonscape features.

**Object 2: THE THREE-DAY-OLD MOON (also visible on Lunar Day 17)**

Our observations begin with the vastness of the oval-shaped **Mare Crisium**, 176km² or, as it is also known, Sea of Crisis, is obscured by the oblique view that it presents to the observer. Having an east–west orientated major axis of 570km, it has a surface area comparable with that of Great Britain. This area is fully visible and easy to identify even though its western half is dark, while its east edge is nearly as bright as the impressive highland regions that border it. Looking to the south of the mare's uplands, a more irregular and less defined plain can be seen.

The vast area of **Mare Fecunditatis** which is crossed by numerous wrinkle ridges, is dominated by the well-known pair of craters **Messier** and **Messier A** [1.9°S, 47.6°E] (as seen in object 2a below), the latter of which is the source of two bright rays radiating to the west, a result perhaps of an oblique meteorite impact. In oblique illumination 'ghost' craters can be seen on the mare surface and also a system of rilles around the crater **Gutenberg** [8.6°S, 41.2°E].

One of the larger craters on display is **Cleomedes**, to the north of Mare Crisium, a distinctive sight with its bright west wall crest and black inner east wall. The crater is often referred to as a Class 5 crater, in the system devised by Ralph Baldwin, who has classified 300 craters. Class 5 type is assigned to those which have undergone various degrees of lava flooding, and are among the older depressions.

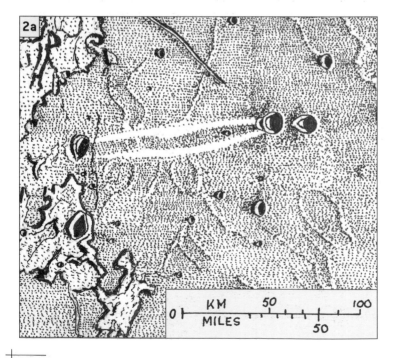

The north-western part of Mare Crisium is encircled by large massifs. Under oblique illumination, numerous wrinkle ridges are prominent on the surface of the Mare. Under high illumination, the rays from the crater **Proclus** [16.1°N, 46.8°E] are prominent.

Worthwhile viewing is the crater **Langrenus** [8.9°S, 60.9°E]; this is a beautiful sight through a telescope. During favourable librations, the dark surface of **Mare Smythii** is visible close to the limb of the Moon [2°S, 87°E].

Moving two diameters of Mare Crisium north west of Cleomedes, is the crater **Endymion** (Class 5), lying on the terminator. With its smooth dark floor, bright west wall and shadow of the east wall, it makes a splendid object. Under oblique illumination a mountain range stands out, forming a nearly continuous wall around Mare Humboldtianum; this wall is partly intersected by a wall of the crater **Belkovich** [61°N, 90°E], which lies in the *libration zone*.

Moving south west of the speck occupied by the one prominent **Petavius** (best seen at two days old) are a pair of much smaller but more easily visible craters, **Stevinus** and **Snellius**, located close to the terminator, and appearing as ellipses rather than circular features, with their bright western walls. These two are worth observing over several nights, as their sharp, distinctive outlines – characteristic of Class 1 craters – become apparent.

Located 46.7°N, 44.4°E is the crater **Atlas**, 87km in diameter which has an unusual floor containing a system of clefts known as Atlas Rimae. In contrast, Atlas has a smaller but prominent neighbour, **Hercules**, characterised by an unmistakable crater on its floor, about 35km in diameter (see object 2b below).

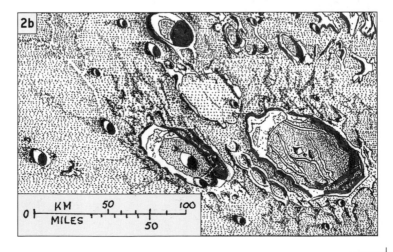

### Object 3: CAPELLA [7.6°S, 34.9°E]

The northern edge of **Mare Nectaris** is accompanied by a prominent pair of craters, **Capella** and **Isodorus**, 49km and 42km in diameter respectively. This pair of craters are one of the brightest objects on the moon and dominate this region. Close to their north-west border located within the **Sinus Asperitatis** is the smaller crater **Torricelli** 23km in diameter, having its open western wall joining up with its smaller neighbour **Censorinus**. Running diagonally from north to east of Capella is a complex system of large rilles with an overall length of 330km and visible even with a modest-sized telescope.

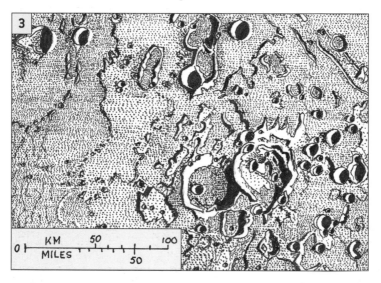

### Object 4: FRACASTORIUS [21.2°S, 33°E]

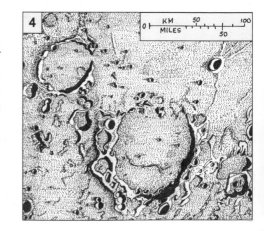

The southern edge of the Mare Nectaris is interrupted by the flooded walled plain of **Fracastorius**, 124km in diameter. To its south is the impressive **Piccolomini** with its 88km diameter terraced walls surrounding a central massif. Observing Fracastorius on the 4th lunar day will reveal its northern wall fragmented and flooded by lava flows, which once filled the central part of the basin Mare Nectaris.

### Object 5: STATIO TRANQUILLITATIS [7°N, 23.5°E]

Located near the southern edge of the **Mare Tranquillitatis** (Sea of Tranquility) is the region of **Statio Tranquillitatis** where on the 20th July 1969 the stillness of billions of years was disturbed when the Apollo 11 Eagle came to rest on a broad level plain, pockmarked with craters ranging from several metres to a fraction of a centimetre across. On this remarkable day, astronauts Armstrong and Aldrin had made history by being the first humans to set foot on the Moon. Their total time spent on the lunar surface was 21 hours 36 minutes and the duration of the moonwalk was 2 hours 31 minutes, in which time they had collected 47.7lb of lunar rock samples. Although there were relatively fresh craters in the area, the astronauts commented that no crater rims were truly sharp. Close to the Apollo 11 landing site (marked with a triangle) are three small craters, **Aldrin**, **Armstrong** and **Collins** (3.4km, 4.6km and 2.4km respectively in diameter). These are the only examples on the nearside of the Moon of lunar formations named after living persons. These craters are seen to their best advantage at sunrise two days before the first quarter and at sunset two days before the last quarter.

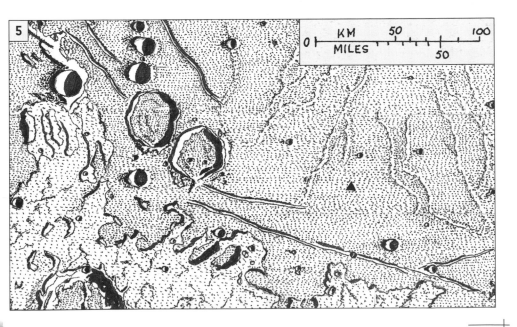

### Object 6: THEOPHILUS [11.4°S, 26.4°E]

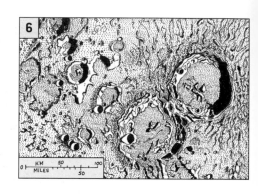

Sited on the southern edge of the uneven surface of the mare region of **Sinus Asperitatis** is the ring mountain **Theophilus**, 100km in diameter. The rim of its walled system has an overall height of 4,400m (almost exactly half the height of Mount Everest) and the summit of the wall rises 1,200m above the surrounding terrain, creating strong dark shadows along its outline. Its unmistakable feature is its 1,400m high *central peak* reflecting the strong sunlight, which stands out against a dark central floor.

The central area also contains the crash landing sites of Ranger 6 and Ranger 8, and the soft landing site of Surveyer 5. South of this region is the awesome sight of **Rupes Altai** (24°S, 23°E), a worthwhile target for the patient observer. Seen at its best at lunar sunset this mountain range resembles a *fault* 480km in length and the strong dark shadows reveal a drop of more than 1,000m throughout its length to the lower lying area.

### Object 7: ARISTOTELES [50.2°N, 17.4°E]

North of the **Montes Caucasus** located in the eastern region of the **Mare Frigoris** (Sea of Cold), lies the beautiful ring mountain **Aristoteles**. Surrounding a small group of central peaks is an extensive system of internal terracing, 87km in diameter. Formed like spokes on a wheel, the immediate external terrain is covered in ejected matter radiating outwards to a distance equal to its own diameter. Lunar sunrise for this location occurs 1.5 days before first quarter, and lunar sunset 1.5 days before last quarter.

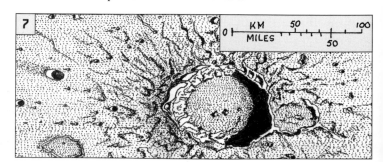

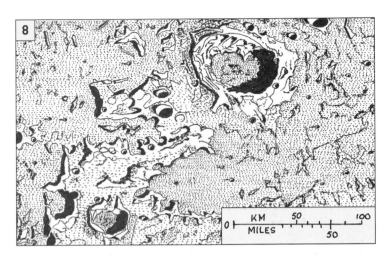

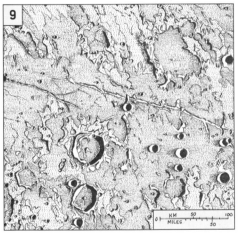

### Object 8: EUDOXUS [44.3°N, 16.3°E]

In contrast to Aristoteles' symmetry and form, **Eudoxus**, 67km diameter, takes on an irregular outline, not surprising given the rugged nature of this region. Extending south south-west from Eudoxus is the impressive Caucasus mountain range which forms a natural boundary between **Mare Imbrium** and **Mare Serenitatis**.

### Object 9: JULIUS CAESAR [9°N, 15.4°E]

Bordered by the Mare Tranquillitatis to its east and **Mare Vaporum** to its west, this 90km flooded crater is characterised by a dark floor and wide walls. Lying to its south-west border is the **Hyginus** region where even the most experienced lunar observer cannot fail to be impressed by the ruggedness of the terrain. Most dominant in this region are the two rilles. The first of these is **Rima Hyginus**, a shallow valley partly formed by a broken overlapping chain of craters 220km in length, providing hard evidence of its violent history. The second is **Rima Ariadaeus**, about twice as wide as Rima Hyginus throughout its 220km length. Both these features are easily observable through small telescopes.

Lying immediately to the south are the relatively small, but nevertheless, impressive craters **Agrippa** and **Godin**, 46km and 35km in diameter respectively. Observed one day before first quarter and at lunar sunset one day before last quarter, their central peaks will not only be shown to full advantage but the entire region will reward the observer with a magnificent lasting impression of the lunar surface.

### Object 10: LINNE [27.7°N, 11.8°E]

The western region of Mare Serenitatis offers, apart from the challenge, crater pits, long wrinkle ridges and, in particular, the mysterious crater **Linne** with a diameter of only 2.4km and, perhaps surprisingly, a depth of 600m. Its main feature in a relatively bare terrain is that it is surrounded by strong ejected material, which under bright sunlight appears through the telescope as a bright spot. Many changes in its appearance were reported in the second half of the 19th century, even its apparent disappearance, but these reports were later explained as classic examples of observing errors.

This mare region, or, as it is sometimes called, the Sea of Serenity, covers a vast area of 303,000km². By comparison, it is similar in shape to Poland, although slightly smaller.

### Object 11: VALLIS ALPES [49°N, 3°E]

Cutting completely through the **Montes Alpes** and bridging the north-eastern corner of the Mare Imbrium to the southern boundary of the Mare Frigoris lies the **Vallis Alpes**, covering an overall distance of 108km. This well-known valley is bordered by steep-sided cliffs which lead to the adjacent mountainous area. This comprises peaks ranging between 1,800m and 2,400m above the nearby Mare Imbrium. The highest mountain **Mons Blanc**, has a height of 3,600m and a base diameter of 25km.

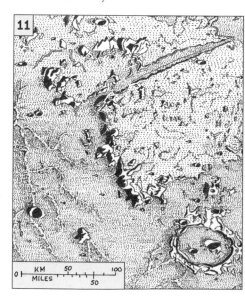

The lunar Alps offer dramatic views, especially at lunar sunrise at first quarter and lunar sunset at last quarter, when long, tapering shadows give a completely false impression of jagged, towering peaks.

Within the same field of view lying at the southern tip of Cape Agassiz (**Promontorium Agassiz** 42°N, 2°E) is the flooded crater **Cassini** with a diameter of 57km. The craters that lie within its relatively shallow walls of 1,240m are **Cassini A**, with a diameter of 17km, and **Cassini B**, with an approximate diameter of 9km.

### Object 12: TRIESNECKER [4.2°N, 3.6°E]

Situated on the relatively smooth floor of **Sinus Medii**, Triesnecker is a prominent crater with a diameter of 26km. Running from the north to south east of Triesnecker for about 225km, and visible through a small telescope, is an area rich in complex sinuous rilles. These are usually 'U' or 'V' shaped in cross section, although in many cases these profiles have been modified by evolutionary processes.

The broken southern boundary lies 200km north of Mare Vaporum [13°N, 3°E] or Sea of Vapours, with a surface area of 55,000km², approximate in size to Lake Michigan in the USA.

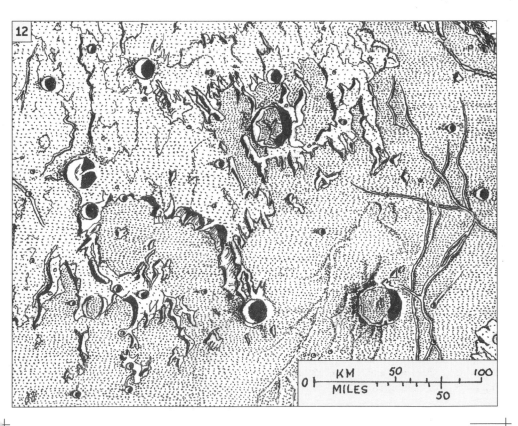

*Left*: The Moon in the first quarter, at seven days old

With the terminator highlighting the nearby surface features, this phase provides an ideal opportunity to get acquainted with the rapidly changing moonscape.

Looking towards the eastern limb, sharp relief gradually gives way to smoothness, presenting the observer with a wide range of objects with which to become familiar. The most striking of these objects is the dark appearance of the lunar maria. If you look at a lunar atlas, you will notice changes in maria appearance, which are due to the effect of libration (see chapter 3). Due to its location Mare Crisium will be particularly affected because of the changing values in libration in longitude.

Other interesting features to observe are the impressive Rupes Altai, the walled plain **Posidonius** (31.8°N, 29.9°E), and the bright ray system eminating from the region of crater Proclus on the western edge of the Mare Crisium. Note also the prominent formation and shadows of Montes Alpes, Montes Caucasus and the **Montes Apenninus**, which can be observed easily with binoculars.

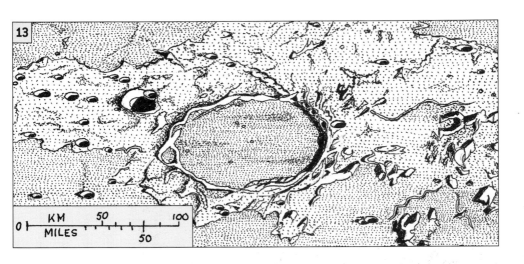

**13**

KM 50 100
0
MILES 50

### Object 13: PLATO [51.6°N, 9.3°W]

A prominent walled plain with a dark floor, visible even through binoculars, is 101km in diameter with an average depth of about 1,000m. Individual mountain peaks, on the eastern and western walls, rise to more than 2,000m above the floor, on which there are four craterlets, about 2km wide (a test for larger telescopes). Sunrise is half a day after the first quarter, sunset half a day after the last quarter.

### Object 14: ARCHIMEDES [29.7°N, 4°W]

A very prominent flooded crater with a diameter of 83km, **Archimedes** has an impressive system of terraced walls. To the north east, almost half way to Cassini, lies the crater **Aristillus**, 53km in diameter with its 3,650m high walls surrounding three central peaks.

The Mare Imbrium (Sea of Rains) has a surface area of 830,000km² and is the largest mare on the Moon's surface: the largest is its adjoining neighbour, **Oceanus Procellarum**. The existence of the basin of the Imbrium is due entirely to an immense impact creating this 1,250km diameter basin during what is known as the **Imbrium Period** (from 3.2–3.8 billion years ago).

A challenge to any observer is to locate **Rima Hadley** [25°N, 3°E], 80km in length. To identify Rima Hadley first locate crater **Conon** [21.6°N, 2°E]. Lying due north of Conon, the distance of crater Archimedes' diameter, Rima Hadley can be found. It nestles in the northern part of the greatest mountain range, which reaches a height of 5,000m above the level of the adjacent maria. Seen through a larger telescope, the Rille Rima Hadley has a width of about 1.5km, a depth of 300m, and is in the vicinity of the Apollo 15 mission landing site.

The lunar Appennines are a magnificent sight at sunset (at last quarter) when their western slopes are illuminated by the Sun.

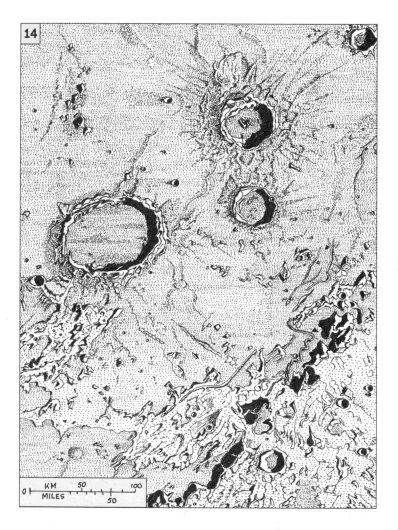

On the 30th July 1971, Apollo 15 landed at the foot of the Appennines close to Rima Hadley (marked with a triangle). Crew members Scott and Irwin spent two days 18 hours and 54 minutes on the lunar surface, completing three moonwalks totalling 18 hours 33 minutes. In a place where previously only shadows moved, they collected 169lb of sample material.

Standing beside the Rover 1, Scott and Irwin looked down the mountainside, with the Hadley rille before them winding into the distance, its walls carving through shadows and sunlight. They could see boulders the size of houses strewn on the valley floor. There was one thing about Hadley they had never anticipated: its spectacular beauty.

### Object 15: PTOLEMAEUS [9.2°S, 1.8°W]

The crater **Ptolemaeus** is situated in the central part of the nearside of the Moon, an area with large, walled plains. The dark surface of Sinus Medii bordered by clefts, extends into this area from the north. This region contains a network of valleys and clefts radiating from the Mare Imbrium.

With prominent terraced walls to the east, Ptolemaeus has an impressive 153km diameter floor with numerous pits and depressions, including the 9km diameter crater **Ammonius** (Ptolemaeus A). Lying immediately to the north is the prominent terraced crater **Herschel**, 41km in diameter. Sharing the Ptolemaeus southern border is the ring mountain **Alphonsus**, which has a central peak on its floor together with floor rilles and crater pits with dark haloes, thought to be pyroclastic vents. It was the crash landing site of the probe Ranger 9.

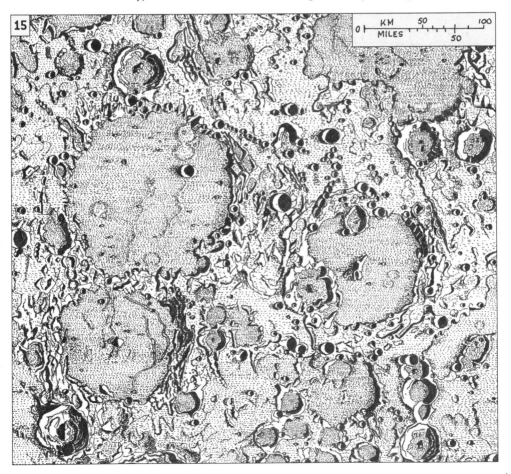

### Object 16: ERATOSTHENES [14.5°N, 11.3°W]

Located at the western edge of the Montes Appenninus, this striking crater, 58km in diameter, has a complex system of terraced walls 3,570m high surrounding central peaks. Under lower lumination, it appears as a defined feature, but at full moon it seems almost to disappear and is as faint as its southern neighbour **Stadius**.

This region's features were once dominated by the debris from the formation of **Eratosthenes**. During what is known as the **Eratosthenian Period** (from roughly 1.0– 3.2 billion years ago) its appearance was quite different from how we see it today, as its ejecta deposits and ray system are now mainly obliterated. The reason for this change is largely due to the later formation of the **Copernicus** crater, with its own deposits and ray system overlaying much of this area. Despite this, the Eratosthenes crater has retained much of its sharp, defining character.

### Object 16: STADIUS [10.5°N, 13.7°W]

A circular depression enclosed with a broken wall 69km in diameter, both its central floor and immediate surrounds have a considerable number of small crater pits, a consequence of material ejected during the formation of Copernicus.

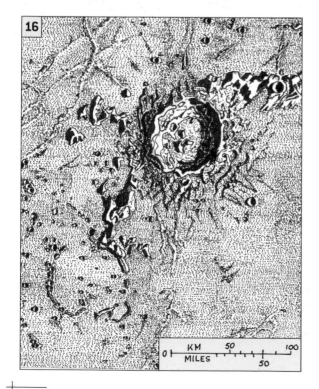

### Object 17: SCHRÖTER [2.6°N, 7°W]

A crater with a considerably disintegrated wall, **Schröter** is open to the south and 34.5km in diameter. Immediately to its south is **Sömmering**, which although slightly smaller, is very similar to Schröter. The two craters are almost connected by **Schröter Rima** [1°N, 6°W]. One theory is that this rille originated as a fault zone and then acted as a channel for lava flow. Although 40km in length, it is not an easy target for observation.

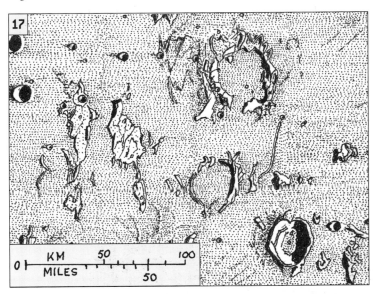

### Object 18: BIRT [22.4°S, 8.5°W]

A prelude to any observing evening are the craters **Birt** (diameter 17km) and **Birt A** (diameter 6.8km), which is located at the edge of Birt's wall. These are situated on the eastern part of the **Mare Nubrium** (Sea of Clouds), with a surface area of 254,000km² and which in itself has many wrinkle ridges. Not far from the crater Birt is **Rupes Recta**, which is a straight wall and the most remarkable fault on the Moon. Technically known as a straight fault, Rupes Recta has a length of 110km with a height of 240–300m, having an apparent width of about 2.5km. When illuminated from the east, it casts a shadow which is easily seen through a small telescope. Rupes Recta does not have a steep slope, as was once believed, but rather a moderate gradient of about 7° and in the setting Sun it takes on the appearance of a fine white line.

It is difficult to imagine the impressive size of such a fault; when compared with an earthly site such as the Niagra Falls, which is seven times shorter and 109 times narrower, you can only wonder at how breathtaking its size would appear to any observer close up.

Immediately north west of crater Birt, larger telescopes will reveal the cleft **Rima Birt**, a rille of about 50km in length which connects the small craters **Birt E**, which is elongated in shape (4.9 x 2.9 km), and **Birt F**, 3.1km in diameter.

About 100km east of Birt is a triple system of craters, consisting of **Thebit the Elder** (57km in diameter) [22°S, 4°W], crater Thebit A (20km in diameter), and **Thebit L** (10km in diameter). You can have some idea of the energy required to create such dramatic terrain if, for example, you consider just one relatively small crater. To produce a 20km diameter crater such as Thebit A you would require a 1km sized meteorite travelling with a cosmic impact velocity of somewhere between 25–30km per second, which is the equivalent energy of a 100,000 megaton bomb.

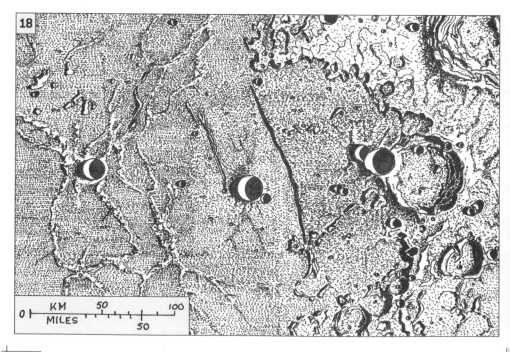

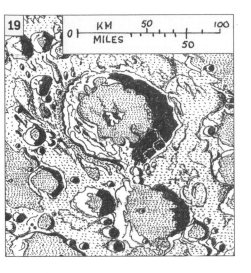

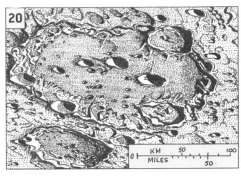

### Object 19: TYCHO [43.3°S, 11.2°W]

**Tycho** is one of the youngest craters on the Moon with an approximate age of 100 million years. It has a diameter of 85km and a surrounding terraced wall with a depth of 4,850m (greater than that of Mont Blanc). Its uneven floor supports a central mountain 1,600m high. Sunrise is one day after the first quarter, sunset one day after the last quarter (see full moon, p.41).

### Object 20: CLAVIUS [58.4°S, 14.4°W]

This is one of the best-known walled plains, 225km in diameter. The small craters inside **Clavius** are suitable objects for testing the resolution of small telescopes. An interesting crescent of craters, decreasing in size, crosses the floor from **Rutherford**. These are **Clavius D, C, N, J, JA**.

# Lunar Days 10 and 25

### Object 21: COPERNICUS [9.7°N, 20°W]

As with all the lunar features we have seen, the approach of the terminator can be likened to a prologue to a theatrical drama. Not only will the spotlight of the Sun show us a backdrop of the Moon's violent geological past, but reveal one of the Moon's principal players, namely the magnificent Copernicus. Thought to be about 900 million years old, it represents a period in lunar history known as the **Copernican Period** (from one billion years ago to the present day).

Here on Earth, our own geological history has been punctuated by several mass extinctions of many species of plants and animals. One such period, known as the **Cenomanian-Turonian boundary** also occurred 90 million years ago. Therefore we can justifiably speculate that cratering activity probably was, and still remains, a common occurrence both on the Earth and the Moon.

Copernicus is a ring mountain and is one of the most prominent centres of bright radiating rays. The terraced walls are elevated 900m above the surrounding terrain, the depth of the crater is about 3,760m, and its diameter is 93km. On the inner side of the walls numerous landslides are visible. The crater's shape is approximately hexagonal. A group of central mountains rise to 1,200m above the floor, which is nearly 25km in diameter. At about nine days old, half the floor is already bright with the terminator passing between the central mountains. The inner west wall is very bright but the central mountain is often difficult to resolve because nearly the whole crater shines so effectively that it reduces the contrast. Bright rays can be traced as far as 800km from the crater. Sunrise is 1.5 days after the first quarter. Sunset is 1.5 days after the last quarter.

To appreciate its size we can compare its awesome features to that of the northern shore of Lake Ontario in Canada where the east–west 44km profile of Toronto sits, with its prominent mile-high CN Tower. A scale comparison (see illustration below) provides a clue to the dramatic energy released when the large meteorite impacted the Moon's surface, creating the Copernicus crater.

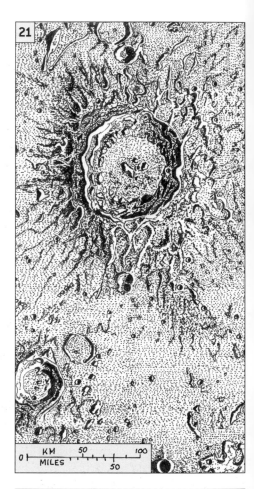

140km south south-west is the prominent crater **Reinhold** [3.3°N, 22.8°W], 48km in diameter with terraced walls 3,260m high.

### Object 22: BULLIALDUS [20.7°S, 22.2°W]
This is a very prominent crater, 61km in diameter with an impressive system of terraced walls, which stand from the crater floor to a height of 3,510m. By comparison Bullialdus is 170m higher than the volcano Mount Etna on the eastern coast of Sicily (Italy). Other points of interest are its central peaks and dramatic radial system surrounding the crater walls.

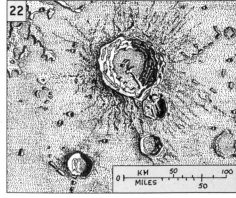

### Object 23: SINUS IRIDUM [45°N, 32°W]

Also known as the Bay of Rainbows, **Sinus Iridum** is a crater formation with a diameter of 260km: equivalent to the distance between London and Manchester. Beyond its northern boundary is the **Jura** mountain range.

### Object 24: LANSBERG [0.3°S, 26.6°W]

A prominent crater 39km in diameter, **Lansberg** is situated in an area containing a number of geologically important locations and, therefore, one of the most observed regions of the Moon.

It was into this area that the probe Ranger 7 crash landed, and where two Apollo expeditions landed: Apollo 12 close to Surveyor 3, and Apollo 14 in the hills at the edge of the crater **Fra Mauro** [6°S, 17°W], best seen on day 10.

The cratered surface at the Apollo 12 site (marked with a triangle) on Oceanus Procellarum was similar to that of Apollo 11, containing craters ranging from very subdued, rimless depressions, to sharp well-defined features containing concentrations of angular blocks. Most of the larger craters near the landing module, ranging from 50–250m in diameter, have subdued rims.

On a previous unmanned orbiter mission, light-coloured material was noticed in the vicinity of the landing site, probably ejected from the impact that formed the large Copernicus crater 230 miles to the north. Part of the astronauts' task was to bring back a sample of this material which would enable geologists to determine the age of this important event in lunar history. It did not take long for the astronauts to make their discovery. As Bean looked at the places where Conrad's boots had dug into the grey soil, he noticed they had uncovered a lighter-grey material just underneath the surface: the very substance they were looking for.

## Object 25: MAIRAN [41.6°N, 43.4°W]

This sharp-rimmed crater is 40km in diameter and is located in the 'continental' area adjoining the Sinus Iridum and reaching south into Oceanus Procellarum. A local curiosity worthwhile observing is a group of peaks to the north of crater **Gruithoisen** [32.9°N, 39.7°W].

The formation **Gruithoisen Gamma** is shaped like an upturned bath tub: in fact, it is a tall dome-like massif with a circular base about 20km in diameter. Domes are manifestations of lunar vulcanism and are observable only when close to the terminator. There is a summit craterlet 900m in diameter which is an ideal test object for larger telescopes.

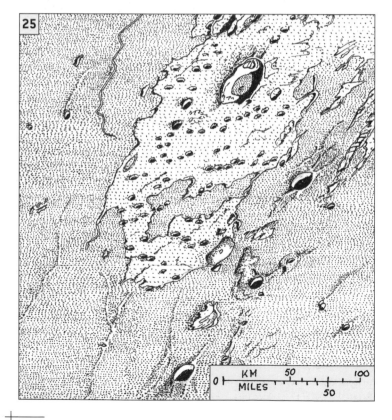

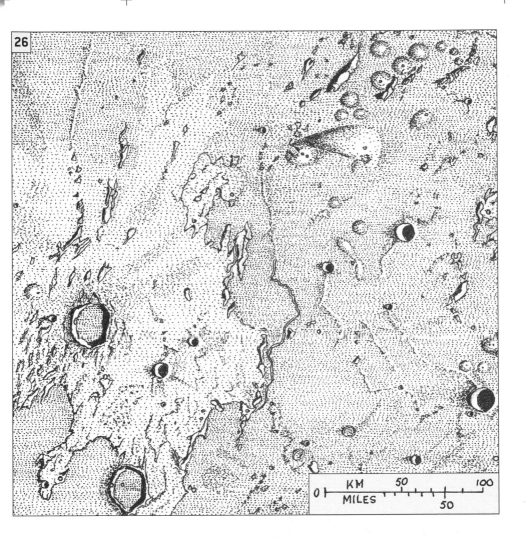

### Object 26: KEPLER [8.1°N, 38°W]

The dark background of the **Mare Insularum** contrasts with the bright ray system from the two main centres: the crater Copernicus (in the east) and, more especially, the crater **Kepler**, 32km in diameter, with an uneven floor, which dominates this area. What could be described as Kepler's identical twin crater lies 80km to the south. This is crater **Encke** [4.6°N, 36.6°W], again with an uneven floor and an overall diameter of 29km. Situated on its western wall is the small crater **Encke N** with a diameter of 3.5km and a depth of 590m. Putting the size of Encke N into perspective, we can compare it with our own well-known meteor crater located between Flagstaff and Winslow, Arizona in the USA, whose impact was felt some

5,000–50,000 years ago and is by comparison a modest 1,700m in diameter and some 180m deep.

Perhaps the best-known group of lunar domes is that situated north of the crater **Hortensius**. Other domes that can be seen through even quite a small telescope lie to the west of the crater **Milichius** and to the south of the crater **T. Mayer**. These very lower formations are observable only in the vicinity of the terminator.

### Object 27: GASSENDI [17.5°S, 39.9°W]

The **Mare Humorum** (Sea of Moisture) is roughly circular in shape with a diameter of 380km, which is equivalent to the distance in Japan between Hiroshima and Kagoshima.

Located at the north-west entrance to the mare is the prominent walled plain of **Gassendi**. Its huge diameter of 110km, Gassendi accommodates central mountains within its walls and a complex system of clefts. Its northern boundary is interrupted by the crater **Gassendi A**, 33km in diameter, with **Gassendi B** neighbouring its north-eastern border.

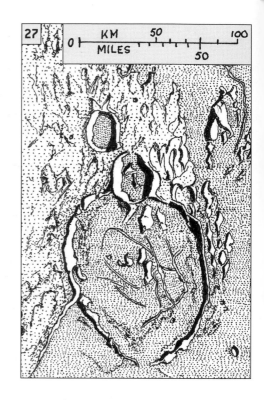

### Object 28: ARISTARCHUS [23.7°N, 47.4°W]

This is one of the brightest objects on the Moon and one of the most conspicuous centres of bright rays. The crater's diameter is 40km, its depth 3,000m. It is so bright that it is clearly visible even on the night side of the Moon in the so-called earthshine.

A number of transient lunar phenomena (TLPs) ,such as hazes and light increases, have been observed in the vicinity of **Aristarchus**. Sunrise occurs almost four days after the first quarter and sunset about four days after the last quarter.

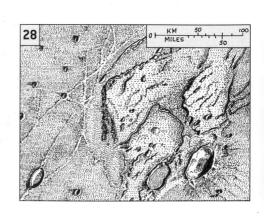

This entire region is rich in features to observe, not least of which is the largest sinuous valley on the Moon, **Schröteri Vallis** [26°N, 51.8°W]. The valley starts 25km north of the crater **Herodotus** and resembles a dry river bed with numerous meanders. Starting at a crater 6km in diameter the valley widens to 10km to form a shape that observers have called the **Cobra's Head**. From this it gradually narrows to 500m and, still narrowing, terminates at a 1,000m high precipice on the edge of a flat-floored valley.

### Object 29: SCHICKARD [44.4°S, 54.6°W]

**Schickard** is a mountainous region along the south-western limb of the Moon, which in the north adjoins the edge of the Mare Humorum. It is one of the largest walled plains, having a diameter of 227km. Its central plains, pot-marked with several craterlets, would prove a challenge to even the most experienced observer. A short distance south of Schickard, about 12km, is the triple system of craters comprising **Wargentin**, **Nasmyth** and **Phocylides**. Viewing at sunrise creates the impression that this system is one crater. This is due entirely to the retreating shadows which give a false impression of walled terracing in the adjoining central area of the craters and disguise its true features.

Patience at the eyepiece will reveal the true identity of craterlets and ridges which form the natural borders between Wargentin, Nasmyth and Phocylides. These are best seen at sunrise 2–3 days before full moon and three days before new moon. Farther south [66.8°S, 69.4°W] is the largest walled plain on the nearside of the Moon, known as **Bailly**. It has a massive diameter of over 303km. Such a large formation is classified as a lunar basin; it has an uneven floor with numerous craters.

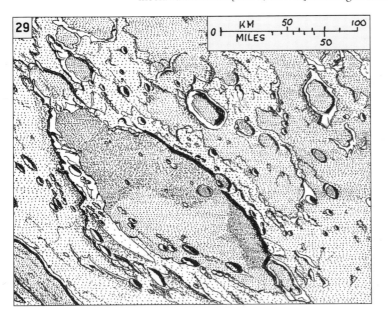

### Object 30: DESCRIPTION OF MAIN FEATURES

It would be wise at this stage in the lunar calendar to fit a a lunar filter to the eyepiece, which will provide considerable eye relief from the lunar glare and without degrading feature details. Located at 66.8°S, 69.4.°W is the vast walled plain Bailly, which is joined with the outer wall of a lunar basin 303km in diameter. Moving to the south-western limb of the Moon, visible even with a small telescope, is a sizeable wide rille called **Rima Sirsalis** [17°S, 62°W].

Continuing northwards on the western limb is the lunar basin **Grimaldi** [5.2°S, 68.6°W], whose flooded centre is surrounded by an inner wall 222km in diameter. The damaged external wall has a diameter of 430km. Immediately to the basin's eastern ridge lies a system of complex rilles about 230km in length. Moving farther north, we pick up the walled plain **Babbage** [59.5°N, 51.3°W], 144km in diameter with the very prominent crater **Pythagorus** [63.5°N, 62.8°W] joining its north-western border.

## Lunar Day 15

### Object 31: THE FULL MOON

Undoubtedly, the most striking features of the full moon are the great ray systems of Tycho and Copernicus. The rays of Tycho present the most dramatic scene, where one can follow a ray right across the Moon's surface, crossing over both light and dark areas, including the Mare Serenitatis, before finally reaching the Moon's limb. This highly illuminated system of rays reaches out, transforming an area of an incredible distance (17 times its own crater diameter) which is the equivalent distance of New York to Cape Canaveral in the USA. In contrast to the bright surface surrounding the crater is a dark ring of materials approximately 150km in diameter. On careful analysis of the rays, you will see a shorter ray originating from the crater **Menelaus** [16.3°N, 16°E] and carrying on to the limb.

One fact that often surprises amateur observers is that one never actually sees a full moon. At full moon, the seen Moon and Earth would be in a straight line, and thus an eclipse would occur. Therefore a 'full moon' will always show some phase at either pole, which makes it an ideal time to observe these neglected regions. The south pole in particular has the sizeable **Leibnitz** mountain range [80°S, 60°E], which can now be seen in profile.

To the east of Bailly you can see some of the brightest mountains on the Moon, rising to 26,000ft. The **Rook** mountains [20°S, 83°W] lie to the west of the crater Schickard. East of the walled plain **Riccioli** [3°S, 74.3°W] you can often see a

*Above*: The full moon

brilliant white and striking object, which is in fact a mountain with a flat top and sloping sides. Under such bright conditions an eyepiece filter will offer the observer eye relief.

A challenge for any lunar observer is to see what can best be described as a chance lunar feature. What is revealed at full moon and for a day or so either side of the full moon is the remarkable image of what appears to be a bold Arabic numeral '6' approximately 560km to the east of the dramatic crater Tycho. The area is generally a somewhat chaotic mixture of dark maria material, and much lighter material, presumably ejected when Tycho was formed. While there are numerous dark patches (for example, the crater **Baracius** and its surroundings, 44.9°S,

16.8°E), the figure runs in an approximate north–south direction across a wide area of ejecta rays which gives it its visibility. Furthermore, by chance two small craters nearby have a higher *albedo* and create the appearance of the centre of the lower 'O' of the figure. Off to the north, light material extending from the east runs westwards just far enough to create the upper part of the figure but not so far as to breach the dark *regolith* which appears to form the upper-left curve of the figure. Its upper-right curve is formed partly by the fortuitous distribution of darker and lighter albedo material, but also by what might be a ridge or old crater rim (this is, incidentally, shown in map XVII of Edmund Neison's classic book *The Moon*, published over 120 years ago).

Finally, try observing the southern area of the Mare Crisium, and endeavour to find a distinct group of white spots, known as the **Trapezium** (not to be confused with M42) or sometimes **Barker's Quadrangle**, named after the lunar observer who first commented on them. Strangely, this group was sometimes omitted from early maps, which has given rise to the idea that they have become prominent only in recent times.

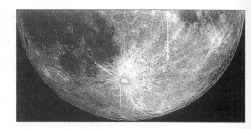

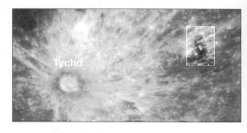

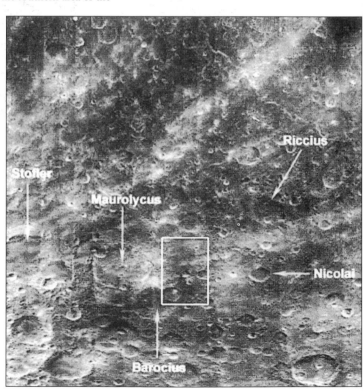

*Right*: The Moon in the last quarter at 22 days old

Appearing in stark contrast against the extensive dark maria background is the ray system that originates from the relatively young craters Copernicus, Kepler and Aristarchus. Dominating the southern hemisphere are the bright rays of crater Tycho and reaching out into the northern hemisphere, and disappearing into the night side of the lunar surface and across the Mare Serenitatis. Due south of Tycho is the extensive walled plain Clavius with the sunrise to its west taking on a different shadowy appearance from when the Moon was nine days old.

The mountain range Montes Jura which borders Sinus Iridum (Bay of Rainbows) can be seen at its best at this time. Following its boundary eastwards towards the terminator, we can follow the outline of the Mare Imbrium and see the unmistakable outlines of Cassini, Aristillus, **Autolycus** and Archimedes.

With practice, patience and attention to detail, finding your way around the Moon's disc and discerning shapes, feature locations, prominent formations and the dark maria, will soon make you a proficient observer as well as being a very rewarding experience.

## INTRODUCTION

In 1609 and 1618 Johannes Kepler announced the three fundamental laws of planetary motion:

1. The planets move in elliptical orbits, the Sun being situated at one focus of the ellipse.

2. The radius vector, an imaginary line joining the centre of a planet to the centre of the Sun, sweeps out equal arcs in equal times (thus a planet moves faster when closer to the Sun).

3. The squares of the 'sidereal periods' of the planets are proportional to the cubes of their mean distance from the Sun.

Given that these laws apply to all bodies in closed elliptical orbits around the Sun, and to satellites orbiting planets, we soon come to realise that an exact description of the Moon's orbital motion is one of the most difficult tasks of theoretical astronomy.

**Kepler's laws** dictate that the Moon's distance from Earth is constantly changing. At *perigee* the Moon's distance from the Earth is 356,400km and the *angular diameter* of its disc is about 33.5' (33.5 minutes) of arc. At *apogee* its distance increases to 406,700km while its angular diameter shrinks to 29.4' (fig 1). By chance, the apparent angular diameter of the Moon is similar to that of the Sun as seen from Earth, about half a degree. With the Moon's distance from Earth being only 30 times the Earth's diameter, one can understand why the Moon exerts such considerable gravitational effect on the Earth,

something we can see in the alternating ebb and flow of the ocean tides. The Earth–Moon system can be regarded as a double planet orbiting around a common centre of gravity which is located 4,700km from the Earth's centre, along a line joining the centres of the two bodies.

Even to the most casual of observers it will be apparent that the Moon always presents the same hemisphere to the Earth. This dynamic property of the Moon's motion is called *synchronous rotation*. It can be seen in (fig 2) that from position 1 to position 2 the Moon completes one quarter of its orbital revolution, while at the same time also turning one quarter of a rotation (90°) on its axis, so that crater A stays in the middle of the side facing the Earth. In the course of one complete orbital revolution, one lunar hemisphere (indicated by the shading) remains hidden from the Earth, although the whole of the Moon is successively illuminated by the Sun. It would therefore be natural to assume that half of the Moon's surface would always be visible to us. Fortunately for us, the dynamics of Kepler's laws permit us to observe some 59% of the total surface area. The benefit to the observer arises from swinging and oscillating motions of the Moon called *librations* and observed here on Earth in the longitude and latitude.

**Libration in longitude** (fig 3) is a direct consequence of Kepler's second law, where the axial rotation of the Moon is constant, while its orbital velocity around the Earth is perpetually changing. The latter reaches a maximum at perigee and then slows down to a minimum at apogee, whereupon it accelerates again, and so on.

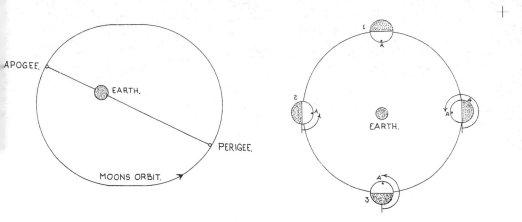

**FIG 1. ELLIPTICAL ORBIT**

**FIG 2. SYNCHRONOUS ROTATION**

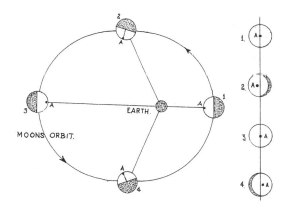

**FIG 3. LIBRATION IN LONGITUDE**

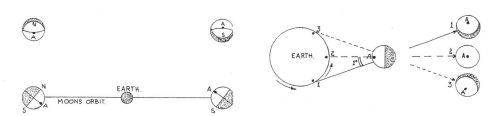

**FIG 4. LIBRATION IN LATITUDE**

**FIG 5. DIURNAL LIBRATION**

For example, from perigee (position 1) the Moon completes one quarter of its orbit around the Earth in less time than it requires for an axial rotation of 90°. This manifests itself by an apparent swinging to the left of the lunar globe, to reveal an area that normally lies beyond the right-hand edge of the Moon. Similarly, from apogee (position 3), the Moon takes longer to reach position 4 than it does to make a quarter of an axial rotation; therefore features that are usually beyond its left-hand edge are brought into view.

**Libration in latitude** (fig 4) is caused by the fact that the Moon's equator is inclined to its orbital plane. This tilt of 6.41° inclines first one pole and then, when the Moon is on the opposite side of its orbit, inclines the other towards the Earth. The rotational axis of the Moon maintains its spatial orientation and points to the same position in space no matter where the Moon is in its orbit. The apparent displacement in latitude amounts to plus or minus 6.50'.

Both librations in latitude and longitude occur simultaneously and continuously and their combined effects bring into view peripheral areas of the Moon's surface called *libration zones*.

Librations in latitude and longitude are of fundamental importance to anyone observing the Moon, so their values are tabulated in most astronomical almanacs. The values of libration in both longitude and latitude on any given day can easily be read off the following monthly libration calendar.

An additional **diurnal libration** (fig 5), amounting to about one degree, arises from the fact that a feature observed on the Moon's surface is seen at slightly different angles from varying viewing locations across the Earth's surface.

In comparing monthly lunar libration values in longitude and latitude, the accompanying libration charts show that marked differences in libration occur from month to month. The purpose of these charts is to allow the observer to identify the ideal viewing dates and favourable libration values when lunar features that normally lie within, or near, the libration zones come into view.

**Example 1 (Longitude):**
The crater **Einstein** (16.6°N, 88.5°W) – which is a walled plain (170km) with a central crater 45km in diameter – lies in a libration zone partly beyond 90°W. Consulting the libration charts for the year 2007 and in conjunction with the lunar day calendar, crater Einstein will be at its best viewing time when the Moon is 15 days old on the following dates where libration values in longitude are at their maximum.

| MONTH | DAY |
|---|---|
| July | 30th |
| August | 28th |

**Example 2 (Latitude):**
The very large crater **Belkovich** (61.5°N, 90°E) is a walled plain with a system of central peaks having two craters on its boundary of 198km diameter. Belkovich lies within the north-eastern libration zone. Consulting the libration chart for the year 2007 and in conjunction with the lunar day calendar, this crater will be best seen when the Moon is two days old on the following date, when values in latitude are at their maximum.

| MONTH | DAY |
|---|---|
| November | 12th |

## KEY

Geocentric: ●—● The markers show 0:00H UT

N. LIMB DISPLAYED

W. (IAV) LIMB DISPLAYED   C. (IAV) LIMB DISPLAYED

S. LIMB DISPLAYED

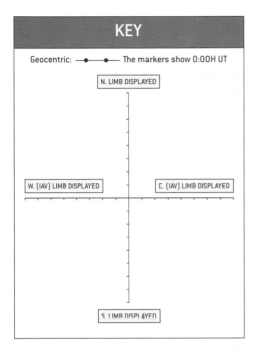

## October

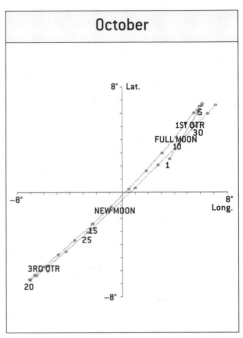

## November

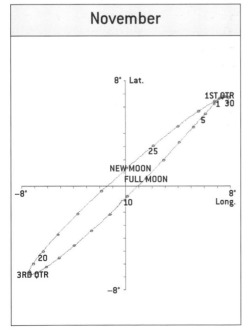

## December

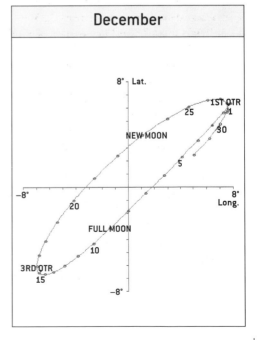

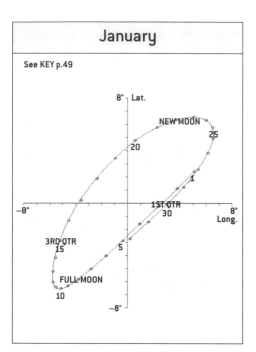

## January

See KEY p.49

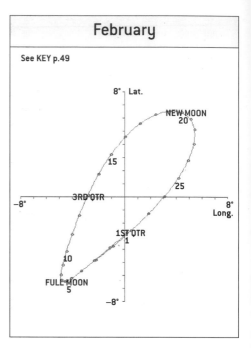

## February

See KEY p.49

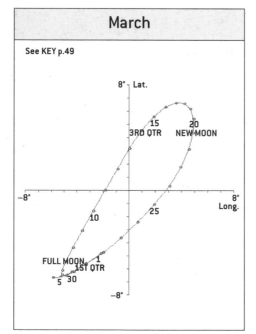

## March

See KEY p.49

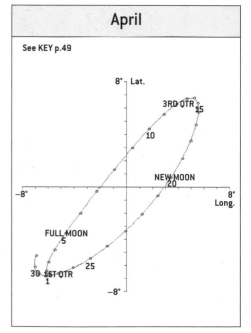

## April

See KEY p.49

## May

See KEY p.49

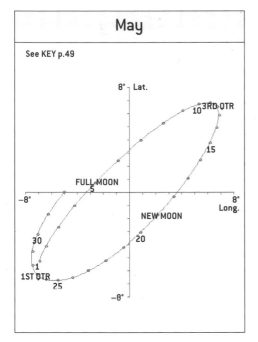

## June

See KEY p.49

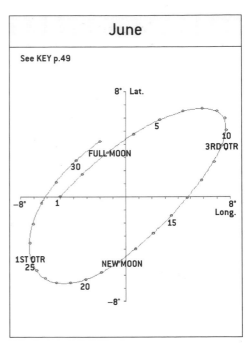

## July

See KEY p.49

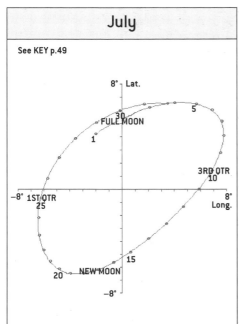

## August

See KEY p.49

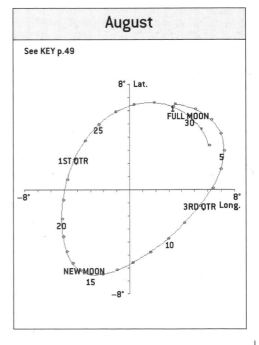

## September

See KEY p.49

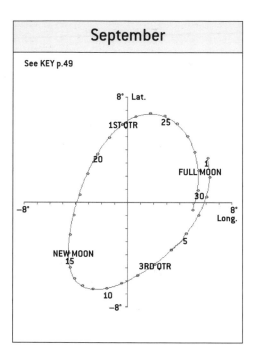

## October

See KEY p.49

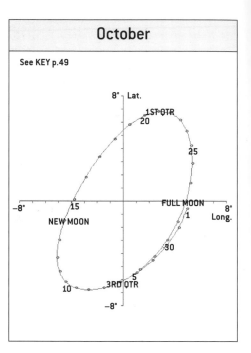

## November

See KEY p.49

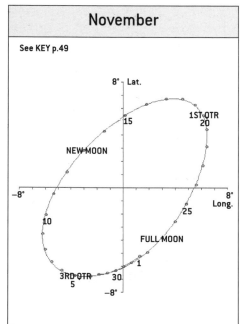

## December

See KEY p.49

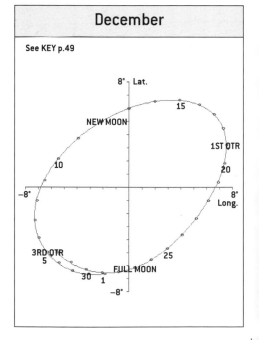

## January

See KEY p.49

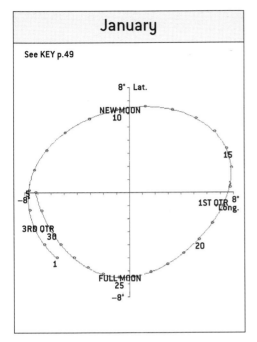

## February

See KEY p.49

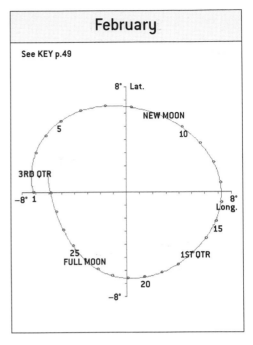

## March

See KEY p.49

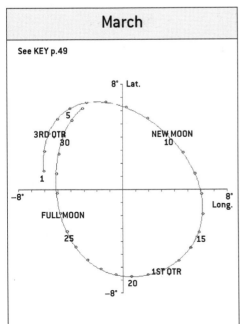

## April

See KEY p.49

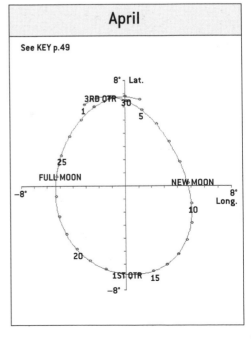

## May

See KEY p.49

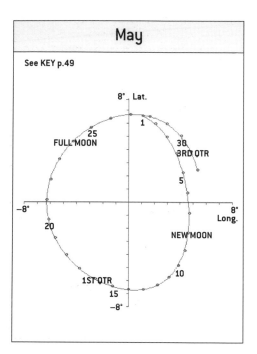

## June

See KEY p.49

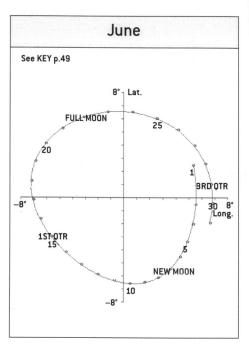

## July

See KEY p.49

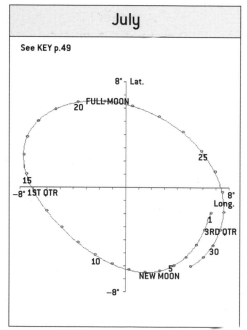

## August

See KEY p.49

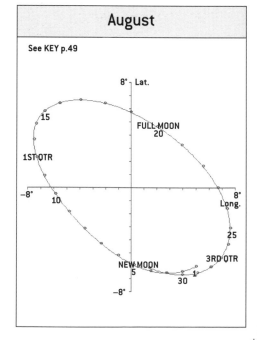

## September

See KEY p.49

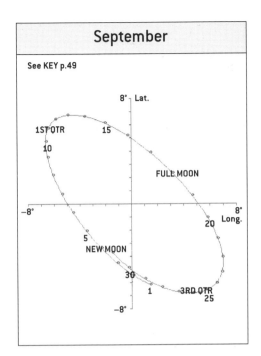

## October

See KEY p.49

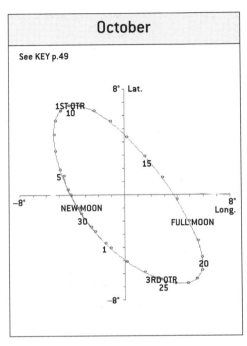

## November

See KEY p.49

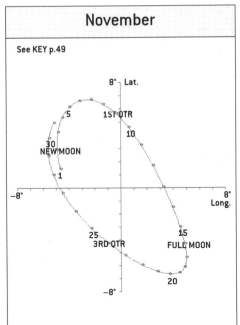

## December

See KEY p.49

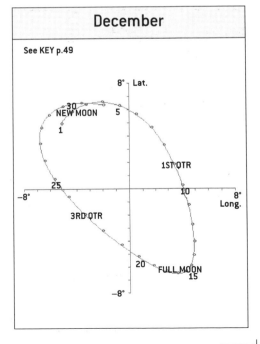

## January

See KEY p.49

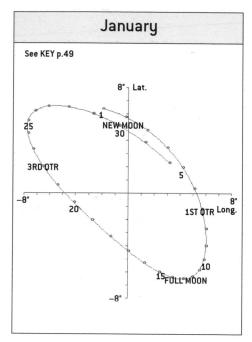

## February

See KEY p.49

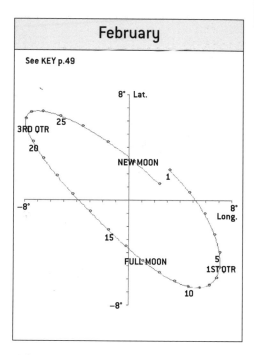

## March

See KEY p.49

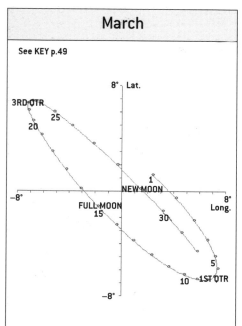

## April

See KEY p.49

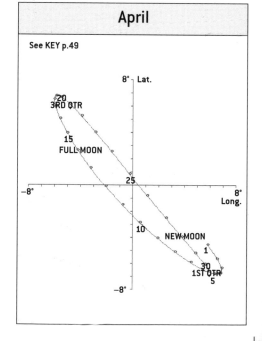

## May

See KEY p.49

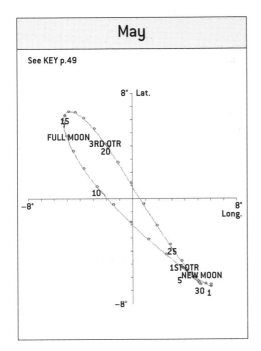

## June

See KEY p.49

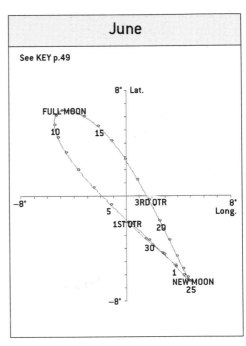

## July

See KEY p.49

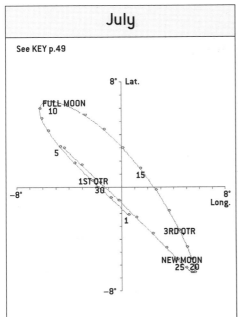

## August

See KEY p.49

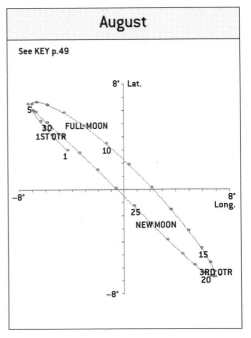

## September

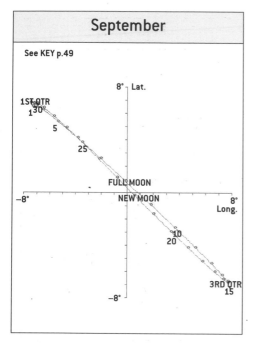

See KEY p.49

## October

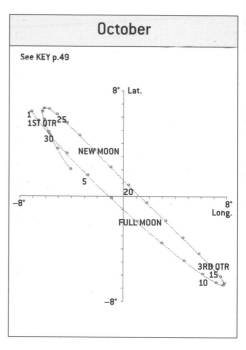

See KEY p.49

## November

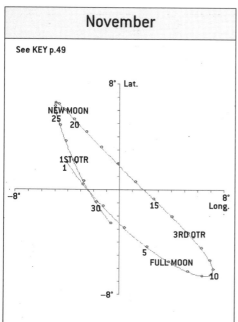

See KEY p.49

## December

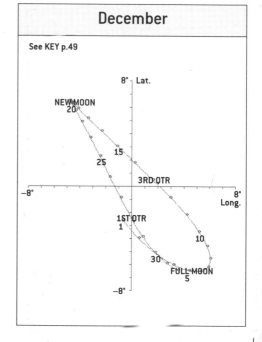

See KEY p.49

## January

See KEY p.49

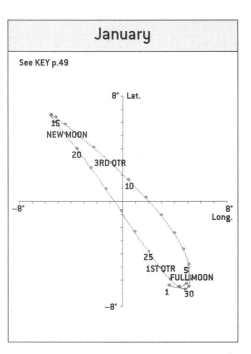

## February

See KEY p.49

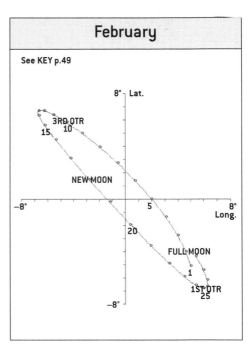

## March

See KEY p.49

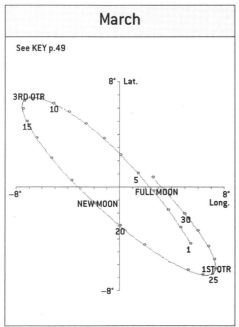

## April

See KEY p.49

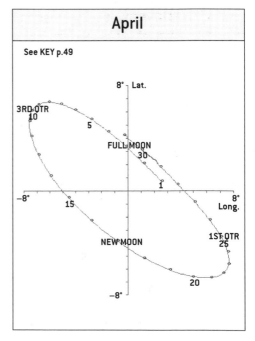

## May

See KEY p.49

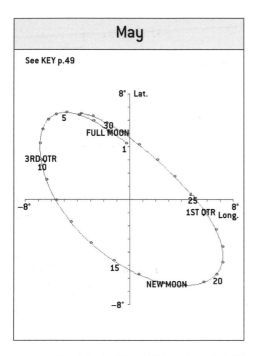

## June

See KEY p.49

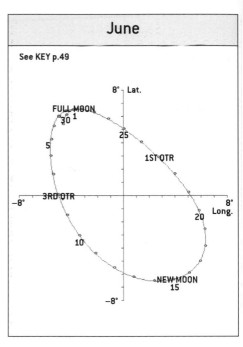

## July

See KEY p.49

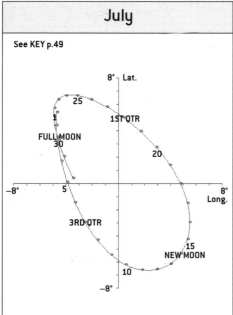

## August

See KEY p.49

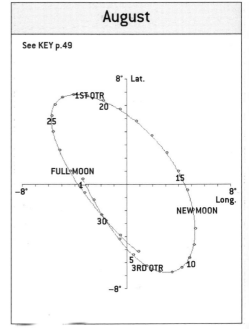

## September

See KEY p.49

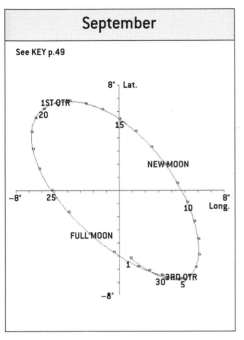

## October

See KEY p.49

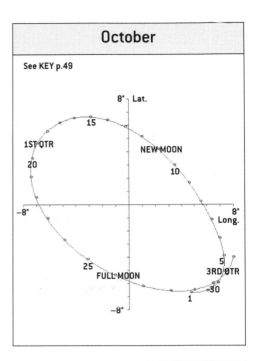

## November

See KEY p.49

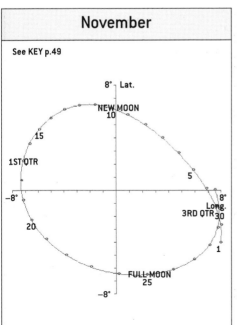

## December

See KEY p.49

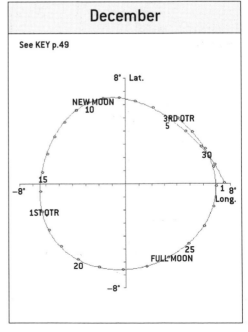

Entry words in the Glossary are italicised in the main text when they first appear in a chapter.

**ACCRETION** The accumulation of gas and dust into larger bodies such as stars, planets and moons.

**AGE OF MOON** The period that has elapsed since the last new moon.

**ALBEDO** The reflectivity of an object, expressed as a ratio of the light it reflects to the light incident upon it and ranging from 1.0 (a white, perfectly reflecting surface) to 0.0 (an absolutely black surface that absorbs all incident radiation).

**APOGEE** The point on the orbit of the Moon (or of an artificial Earth satellite) when it is furthest from the Earth.

**BASALT** Igneus rock, solidified lava or *magma*, fine grained, and black or dark grey in hue. Various kinds were found on the Moon and also exist on the other terrestrial planets: Mercury, Venus and Mars.

**BRECCIA** Rock composed of broken rock fragments welded together by the extreme heat and pressure of a meteoroid impact.

**CENTRAL PEAK** The mountain or group of mountains at the centre of a large *impact crater*.

**CRATER** A circular depression, usually with an elevated wall. These formations are found on cosmic bodies with solid surfaces, most notably planetary moons.

**CRATER, IMPACT** (Also called *meteorite crater.*) A *crater* formed by the impact of a meteoritic body or, in the case of secondary craters, by the *ejecta* from such impacts.

**DIAMETER, APPARENT** (Also called *angular diameter.*) The diameter of a celestial object expressed in angular measure. For example, the apparent diameter of the Moon is about 30' (0.5°).

**ECCENTRICITY** One of the elements of an eliptical orbit of a celestial body, it is the elongation of the ellipse, obtained by dividing the distance between two focal points by the major axis. The eccentricity, e = o for a circular orbit. For an elliptical orbit, e lies between 0 and 1.

**ECLIPTIC** The apparent orbit of the Sun around the celestial sphere. The Sun appears to complete one circuit along the ecliptic in one year.

**EROSION** Disintegration of a lunar or planetary surface caused by natural forces, for example water, wind, and frost. On celestial bodies without atmospheres, such as the Moon, erosion is caused mainly by the impacts of meteorites and *micrometeorites*.

**ESCAPE VELOCITY** (Also called *parabolic velocity* or *the second cosmic velocity.*) The minimum velocity that a body has to attain to escape from a gravitational field of a more massive body, such as a planet.

**FAULT** A fracture in the crust at which one side has moved relative to the other.

**FOCUS** The point to which a parallel beam of light entering an optical system axially, is refracted or reflected to form a sharply defined or focused image.

**LIBRATION** The lunar librations in latitude and longitude are the apparent vertical and horizontal rocking motions of the Moon as it orbits the Earth. Their combined effect enables us to observe rather more than 50% of the Moon's surface over a period of time.

**LIBRATION ZONES** Peripheral areas of the lunar surface that are alternately turned towards and away from the Earth as a result of the lunar *librations*. The approximate longitudinal centres of these zones are the meridians 90°E and 90°W.

**LINE OF NODES** The line joining the two points where the Moon's orbit intersects the *ecliptic*, to which it is inclined by 5°. The point at which the Moon crosses the ecliptic from south to north is termed the 'ascending node'. Similarly, the point at which it crosses it moving it from north to south is termed the 'descending node'. The line of nodes continually changes its orientation in space, but returns to the same points of intersection with the ecliptic every 18.61 years.

**LUNAR RAYS** Diverging for typical distances of 10 diameters from well-formed young *craters*, these systems of straight or curved streaks look like splash marks. Many rays traverse relief without deviation or interruption. Most rays are brighter than the underlying rocks, although some minor rays are darker. The exceptional Tycho has ray extending to 23 diameters (2,001km). Some rays form ovals and others seem to follow the crests of ridges. Many apparently continuous rays resolve into linear elements which point only roughly towards the centres of their parent craters. The rays are widely thought to be surficial deposits of finely comminuted ballistic ejecta from craters. But rays also contain small craters and blocks and ray-elements commonly fan out from these secondary craters.

**LUNATION** The *synodic month*, which is the time taken by the Moon to complete on set of phases; for example, from new moon to new moon it takes 29 days 12 hours 44 minutes 2.8 seconds.

**MAGMA** Subterranean molten rock which emerges as lava during volcanic eruptions.

**MARE** (pl. **MARIA**) Any of several dark and relatively smooth regions on the Moon (and Mars) that are composed of basaltic flows.

**MASCON** Abbreviated form of the term *mass concentration* which refers to denser material under the lunar *mare* basins that was manifest by local anomalies in the Moon's gravitational field. The mare basins, which were formed more than 4,000 million years ago, contain solidified *magma* to considerable depth and this is thought to be responsible for these anomalies.

**MICROMETEORITE** A meteorite particle less than a millimetre in diameter.

**MONTH, ANOMALISTIC** The time that elapses between two successive orbital passages of the Moon through *perigee*: 27 days 13 hours 18 minutes 33.1 seconds. Since the perigee is successively displaced in the direction of the Moon's motion, the Moon describes an angle of slightly more than 360° during a normalistic month. This is why an anomalistic month is longer than a *sidereal month*.

**MONTH, SIDEREAL** The time taken by the Moon to complete one revolution around the Earth with respect to the background stars: 27 days 7 hours 45 minutes 11.5 seconds.

**MONTH, SYNODIC** (See also *lunation*.) The time taken by the Moon to complete one set of *phases*, for example from new moon to new moon.

**PERIGEE** The point on the orbit of the Moon (or of an artificial Earth satellite) where it is closest to the Earth.

**PHASE** The amount of the illuminated disc of a dark body, such as the Moon, which shines by reflected sunlight that is visible from Earth. It depends on the ever-changing angle between the Sun, the dark body and the Earth. The main lunar phases are: new moon, first quarter, full moon and last quarter.

**PHASE ANGLE** The angle between the Sun, an object and an observer.

**REGOLITH** The incoherent surface layer of the Moon and many other bodies in the Solar System that do not have a protective atmosphere. It consists of crushed and fragmented rocks, resulting largely from millions of years of meteorite impacts. The lunar regolith is said to have a depth of about 10–100m.

**RILLE** Any of various long, narrow, straight depressions on the Moon's surface, hundreds of kilometres long and 1–2km wide.

**ROCHE LIMIT** A satellite orbiting close to its planet is subjected to great stresses as the nearer portions try to orbit faster than the more distant parts. If close enough, these stresses exceed the strength of the rock and the satellite will be ripped apart. Alternatively, it will never be able to form by the *accretion* process. The Roche limit is the critical distance from the planet, usually quoted as 2.5 times the planet's radius, though the exact number depends on the composition of both bodies. For example, the rings of Saturn lie within its Roche limit.

**ROTATION, CAPTURED OR SYNCHRONOUS** The axial rotation of a satellite in a period equal to the time of the revolution around its primary, so that it always presents the same hemisphere (as in the case of our Moon). It is a consequence of the action of *tidal forces* between two bodies.

**RUPES** Ridges or cliffs on planetary surfaces.

**SCARP** A sharp break between two surfaces, usually developed by *erosion* along a boundary between lithologies of differing resistance, or a *fault* line.

**TERMINATOR** The boundary between light and shadow, or between day and night, on a body that does not shine by its own light. In the case of the Moon, the morning terminator heralds sunrise; the evening terminator is the beginning of the 14-day-long lunar night.

**TIDAL FORCES** The mutual gravitational forces between two or more neighbouring cosmic bodies, which can deform their shapes and, in extreme cases, can cause their disintegration. Familiar terrestrial phenomena are the tides caused by the attraction of the Sun and Moon.

**TIDAL HEATING** The frictional heating of a satellite's interior caused by repeated flexure induced by the gravitational field of its parent planet.

**VOLATILES** Elements or compounds with low melting temperatures, such as potassium, sodium, water and ammonia.

# REFERENCES

E. Uchupi & K.O. Emery, *Morphology of the Rocky Members of the Solar System* (Springer-Verlag Berlin and Heidelberg GmbH & Co., 1993)

Grant Heiken, David Vaniman & Bevan M. French, *Lunar Source Book* (Cambridge University Press, 1991)

Antonìn Rükl & Thomas W. Rackham, *Atlas of the Moon* (Kalmbach Publishing Company, 1996)

Andrew Chaikin, *A Man on the Moon* (Penguin, 1995)

J. Kelly Beatty & Andrew Chaikin, *The New Solar System* 3rd Edition (Cambridge University Press, 1999)

*Astronomy & Geophysics: The Journal of the Royal Astronomical Society*, February 2001 Vol 42, Issue 1

Patrick Moore, *Astronomy Encyclopedia* (Mitchell Beazley, 1987)

## ACKNOWLEDGEMENTS

I am deeply grateful for the kind permission granted to me from the following people to use their material in this book: Mr H.J.P. Arnold, Consultant, Space Flight-Astro Imaging photography for his figure '6' feature on the Moon; and Mr J.M.H. Hill for the diagrams from his Libration Program. My grateful thanks to my wife Irene, for all the typing and patience needed in compiling this book.

## ABOUT THE AUTHOR

John S. Folkes is a Fellow of the Royal Astronomical Society, and a regular guest speaker at many local astronomical societies. He is passionate about promoting astronomy in schools and helps to familiarise amateur observers with lunar features through his spectacular illustrations. John is now retired and lives near Aylesbury, Buckinghamshire with his wife, Irene. This is his first book.